'Seeing the Big

How God Restores the Human Soul.

By

Rev D Kevin Jones B.A. M.A

To my brother Meyrick and sister Catherine.

Published by

"Heart of Oak" 22 Chapel Lane, Banks, Southport, Lancashire, England, PR9 8EY.

heartofoak@safe-mail.net

Tel: 44 (0)1704 228394
ISBN> 0-9549462-6-X

First Edition published in United Kingdom 2010.

Printed and bound by: Lightning Source UK LTD. 6 Precedent Drive, Rooksley, Milton Keynes, Bedfordshire, MK13 8PR.

Introduction.

So many things demand attention in our busy lives, that
sometimes it is hard to keep the main thing as the main thing.
God still has a wonderful plan for His people; He is seeking to remake us in the lost image of son ship.

As a youth, we think we have all the time in the world; as we
grow older our priorities change. This book is for those who no
longer want to paddle in spiritual pools but are seeking to walk
closer with God, the Father, Son and Holy Spirit. It is a journey I
am still engaged in and as I progress I am finding that only Jesus
satisfies; anything that seeks to usurp His place is ultimately
unsatisfying.

God is in the process of re-forming us in our inner being in the
image of His Son Jesus Christ. As Christians we are by nature
spiritual beings, but so few of us know how to draw on the
resources of the Eternal Spirit. I believe God begins to restore us
by flooding our Spirit with the presence of His Holy Spirit. The
Holy Spirit then begins to reshape our Soul (our personality, and
character, our mind and heart) and remoulds us according to
God's original design. As the Soul is remade in the image of its
creator God's love and power then overflow in to the body.

This book seeks to identify the need of the human soul and show how God is seeking to 'restore our souls.' Many Christians talk about a relationship with Jesus but practice a religion. Religion can never restore the soul; this is only accomplished through a deep relationship with the Holy Spirit. If we are God's children then we have the right to walk in the presence of our Father. We are not primarily servants, but sons and daughters of the living God. The Scripture says *'If we live in the Spirit, let us also walk in the Spirit.' Gal 5:25 KJV.* The aim of this book is to help us walk in the Spirit. It looks at both the theology and practice of walking with God.

Contents.

1: Seeing the Big Picture.

The Sistine chapel ceiling contains one of the most famous pictures ever painted, the picture of the hand of God reaching out to Adam. The two hands are perpetually frozen just millimetres apart. Yet this often reproduced image is just part of the whole and if we were to concentrate on this one small picture we would miss the glory of the 'BIG PICTURE'. Anyone walking into the Sistine Chapel would not simply see the central motif of the creation of Adam. They would find their senses assailed by a riot of colour and could spend hours drinking in the depth and grandeur of the story unfolded before their eyes. The truth is that the little picture is only explained adequately when it is set in the context of the Big Picture. The same is true of our lives: when we concentrate on the little picture, the immediate problem or situation we are facing, we do not appreciate the full glory of God's plan for our lives. It is only as we see God's over riding plan that our own lives are set in context. When we see the Big Picture we begin to understand who we are and why we were created. We see that we are part of something greater and grander than we can imagine. In life it is easier to concentrate on one small part, but if we get caught up in our little drama we can miss the big picture that is at work around and within us.

The Bible paints in mammoth brush strokes as well as tiny details. It gives us a background of the creation and fall, the lost spiritual standing and ultimate salvation, restoration, and renewal of mankind.

The Creation.

Here we are concerned with the large brush strokes not the infinite details which are also important. Perhaps the two most important phrases in the creation account are: *'So God created* **man in His own image***; in the image of God He created him; male and female He created them. Then God* **blessed** *them.'* Gen 1:27-28 NKJ; and Gen 1:31 *'Then God saw everything that He had made, and indeed it was* **very good***. So the evening and the morning were the sixth day.'* Gen 2:3 *Then God* **blessed** *the seventh day and sanctified it.'* NKJ

A picture we are presented in the first two chapters of Genesis is one of pristine innocence and sublime beauty. The earth and mankind are perfect, but that perfection is yet to be put to the test. This is a world bathed in the Love and pleasure of God. The first picture we need to fasten firmly in our minds is that God deeply loves His creation. Again and again we are told that God blessed His creation and that God was not simply pleased with His work; His assessment was that it was 'very good' *Gen 1:31 'And God saw every thing that he had made, and, behold, it was*

very good. And the evening and the morning were the sixth day.'
KJV

Next we come to the **unique** nature invested in mankind at our creation. This is the mystery: *God creating man in His own image.* Mankind is distinguished from any other created being in that we bear the divine image. We are not talking about the physical image of God, Christ alone is God in the flesh, but we are talking of the spiritual, emotional and psychological image of God. Mankind alone is a three part being, and whatever we think being made in God's image means, we can guarantee that our thoughts are not big enough.

Firstly, we bear a Trinitarian likeness. God is a three personal being; this concept is latent though not explicit in the creation account. The first two verses of Genesis One introduce us to God as Elohim. This is the most ancient name for God. [El is the singular form and was used by many nations not just the Hebrews. Eloah is the plural form of the name used to show God's greatness, and is often in the vocative as a form of address or worship. Elohim is the straight plural for God and means God, more than two]. Genesis records '*In the beginning God [Elohim] created the heavens and the earth. The earth was without form, and void; and darkness was on the face of the deep. And the*

Spirit of God was hovering over the face of the waters. Then God said, "Let there be light"; and there was light.' Gen 1:1-2. With the light of the New Testament scriptures we begin to see a fuller picture of the nature of God. He is depicted here as the Creator, [in the beginning God] as Spirit [the spirit of God hovering over the waters] and Word, [then God said]. At the outset we have one God depicted in the plural one who is who is more than two persons in nature.

C S Lewis, in his book Mere Christianity, begins to define the nature of this tripartite God. "A good many people nowadays say, 'I believe in a God, but not in a personal God.' They feel that the mysterious something which is behind all other things must be more than a person. Now the Christians quite agree. But the Christians are the only people who offer any idea of what a being that is beyond personality could be like. All the other people, though they say that God is beyond personality, really think of Him as something impersonal: that is, as something less than personal. If you are looking for something super-personal, something more than a person, then it is not a question of choosing between the Christian idea and the other ideas. The Christian idea is the only one on the market. "

Now if God is a three personal being and we are made in His image we should expect that we also are three part beings, consisting of BODY, SOUL and SPIRIT. This differentiates from the plant kingdom which has a body but no soul, and the animal kingdom which has body and soul but no eternal spirit.

We must also understand that God is a relational being. God exists in a self giving eternal relationship between the persons of the trinity. God in His very core is relational and this means that we are made to relate, firstly to God and then to each other. God is a community and we are made for community. This emerges in the Genesis account where God says *'It is not good that the man should be alone.' Gen 2:18 KJV.* God is a family, and self-giving love binds the eternal relationship of Father, Son and Holy Spirit. Therefore as people created in His image the need for relationships is imprinted on our inmost being.

What else is God like? The scripture gives us many insights into His nature. God is eternal and we are told, He *'has also set eternity in the hearts of men.' Eccl 3:11.*
- *God **is love** 1 John 4:16.*
- *God **is holy** Ps 99:9.*
- *God **is righteous** Dan 9:14.*
- *God **is faithful** 2 Cor 1:18.*
- *God is **not unjust** Heb 6:10.*
- *God is **sovereign** Dan 5:21.*

As His image bearers possessing His moral, spiritual and psychological characteristics, we are made for love, holiness, righteousness, faithfulness and justice. That is why our souls recoil form hatred, unfaithfulness, unrighteousness and injustice. As His emissary man was made to rule with Godly wisdom and compassion over this earth. This was the condition of the initial creation and with such a creation God was genuinely pleased.

The fall.

Gen 2:16-17 "And the LORD God commanded the man, "You are free to eat from any tree in the garden; but you must not eat from the tree of the knowledge of good and evil, for when you eat of it you will surely die."

When mankind disobeyed God's command they entered into the experience of both good and evil. Knowledge in the Bible is never an academic understanding, but and experiential reality. To know both good and evil means to experience both good and evil. Just as when the Bible tells us Adam knew his wife, it meant he was intimately acquainted with her, so when it says we would know evil it means we would become intimately acquainted with evil. Knowledge and experience are not separated in the human condition. The curse of this world is that we live under the experience of good and evil. This is a picture of our world today.

We understand and appreciate that which is good, but we turn too often towards evil. St Paul put it this way, *'what I do is not the good I want to do; no, the evil I do not want to do-- this I keep on doing.' Rom 7:19* God's intention was for mankind to mirror his experience and carry only good within the soul, but disobedience corrupted the inner being so that each of us is a mix of good and evil.

The breakdown in our inner being goes further for we were promised that *'"when you eat of **it you will surely die**."* The experience of sin and death entered into our beings. The New Testament underlines this: *1 Cor 15:21-22, '**death came through a man**, for as **in Adam all die**, so in Christ all will be made alive.'*

1.   As a result of our fallen condition **the body** ages and dies. Disease, pain, hard labour and ultimately death are a result of the fall.

2.   Though physical death took many years, **Spiritual death** was immediate. We see it in the relationship with God, Adam is now hiding from and fearful of his creator. This is why we need a spiritual re-birth. The Spirit of God that was breathed into Adam at creation - *Gen 2:7 'The LORD God formed man of the dust of the ground, and breathed into his nostrils the breath of life; and*

man became a living soul' – that living Holy Spirit no longer
dwells within the fallen human spirit. We are spiritually dead.

In order for us to be fully alive, God has to restore the spiritual life
within, but as long as we are un-repentant and living under the
dominion of sin He cannot. Spiritual life is drawn from God
Himself and unless we are cleansed we cannot draw life from a
Holy God. [The indwelling Holy Spirit will not dwell richly in an
unholy human spirit.]

3.   What about **the Soul**? We often miss the effect the fall
has on our soul, our personality, emotional and mental make up.

a.   Our relationships are profoundly affected, by the fall.
Rather than loving and protecting each other, Adam and Eve
sought to protect themselves by shifting the blame. They
became profoundly self-centred. Their moral integrity was
infected by sin at every level. [The doctrine of Original Sin does not
teach that mankind is as thoroughly wicked as he can be, rather it
teaches us that there is no part of our personality that has not been
tainted by sin.] Our love and our relationships are self-centred,
our personalities are self-serving, we take more than we give.
We are insecure and blame others. We have a deep seated
need to be loved but somehow find selfless love so difficult. We

14

exchange lust for love and parade faithfulness as a virtue. We find it hard to trust and when we do we are so often let down.

b.   Sin also affects our COMMUNITIES; we become isolated and suspicious, we divide ourselves by colour, race, county and religion. As relational beings, we were made to relate deeply trustingly and lovingly to other people, but our communities are infected with suspicion, mistrust and hate. One of the reasons God gave the 10 commandments was to limit the effects of sin in society. God can no longer look at our communities and lives, say that is good, and then add His blessing.

The picture we are given is no longer of mankind bearing God's image but of us bearing the image of Adam. *Gen 5:1-3 'When God created man, he made him **in the likeness of God**. He created them male and female and blessed them. And when they were created, he called them "man". When Adam had lived 130 years, he had a son in his own likeness, **in his own image.**'*

The Big Picture tells us that we are fallen creatures who are profoundly affected by sin on a physical, spiritual, moral and social level.

What is God doing to rectify the situation?

The answer is that He begins with a spiritual rebirth through repentance and faith. He then sets about remaking our inner being in the image of His Son Jesus. This is God's restoration project, *Ps 23:3 'He restoreth my soul.'* He will finally through the resurrection renew the body. God's plan is to remake mankind not in the image of Adam who fell, but in the image of Christ who succeeded. It is a whole plan for the whole person, Spirit, Soul and Body.

In this spiritual renewal, God is beginning to rebuild our lives, renewing the lost image, from the inside out. We receive spiritual renewal that leads to psychological and moral renewal. *Rom 8:10 'if Christ is in you, your body is dead because of sin, yet your spirit is alive because of righteousness.'* Once The Spirit of God, is again dwelling at the heart of the human personality, He will begin to reshape us into the people God intended us to be. God works from the inside out, indwelling the spirit, flooding out into the soul and finally directing and guiding the body. As believers we are not three separate beings, body, soul and spirit in opposition to one another, but one being living in harmony with the indwelling Holy Spirit of God.

In order to find this spiritual renewal the first two building blocks we need are **repentance and faith** towards God. *'Therefore let us leave the elementary teachings about Christ and go on to maturity, not laying again **the foundation of repentance** from acts that lead to death, **and of faith in God.**' Heb 6:1*

In the Old Testament we are taught of the nature of sin through the sacrificial system. The worshiper would acknowledge their sin as they came through the blood of a sacrifice; before someone could worship God sin was always covered by blood. It was always so. The book of Leviticus gives us great detail about what sacrifices are acceptable. In the New Testament we learn that God did not require the sacrifice of bulls and goats but through these means He was teaching them that sin deserved death. *"Sacrifice and offering You did not desire, But a body You have prepared for Me. In burnt offerings and sacrifices for sin You had no pleasure. Then I said, 'Behold, I have come-- In the volume of the book it is written of Me--To do Your will, O God.' Heb 10:5-7 "NKJV* Just as the lamb of the Old Testament was a substitute and sacrifice for the sinner who approached God, so Jesus in His death has become our substitute and sacrifice.

If we are to trust in His offering on our behalf we need both **repentance and faith**. Faith alone can lead to presumption;

repentance alone can lead to introspection. It is only when we humble ourselves as sinners and look up to the sure sacrifice of Jesus that we have assurance of forgiveness. Repentance and faith put us in a place where we can again share in the spiritual life of God. When we come to Christ in repentance and faith we are re-born and renewed; this is why many people feel a great sense of joy and assurance. They are spiritually alive and have a new relationship with God. The source of eternal life is restored. God begins working on the inside but it then flows out from the centre of their being.

HE BEGINS THE PROCESS of restoring our souls, *Col 3:9-10* *'you have taken off your old self with its practices and have put on the new self, which is **being renewed in knowledge in the image of its Creator**.* This is called discipleship, as Christ restores our personality and remakes us in His own image.

He affects our relationships; we now have the choice to react either in the flesh or in the Spirit. **Spiritual life should now flood into our family life,** as we learn to love in a non-selfish way. Rather than blaming each other we begin to forgive and forget. Some Christians never allow the renewed self to affect their thoughts, actions and relationships. They stop at being 'Born again' but never see the 'restored soul'. We can either act in accordance with our feelings or act in accordance with the truth of God's word and begin to LOVE as Christ loves, without finding faults or belittling each other. The New Testament is full of instructions to new Christians on how to live; again we find that doctrine is never meant to be head knowledge but to produce heart knowledge.

'If you have any encouragement from being united with Christ, if any comfort from his love, if any fellowship with the Spirit, if any tenderness and compassion, then make my joy complete by being like-minded, having the same love, being one in spirit and purpose. Do nothing out of selfish ambition or vain conceit, but in humility consider others better than yourselves. Each of you should look not only to your own interests, but also to the interests of others. Your attitude should be the same as that of Christ Jesus:' Phil 2:1-5

How we deal with disagreements will demonstrate the depths of our Christian faith. *Eph 4:32 'Be kind one to another, tender-hearted, forgiving one another, even as God for Christ's sake has forgiven you. KJV m. Col 3:8-10 'But now you must rid yourselves of all such things as these: anger, rage, malice, slander and filthy language from your lips. Do not lie to each other, since you have taken off your old self with its*

19

practices and have put on the new self, which is being renewed in knowledge in the image of its Creator.' (NIV) If our doctrine does not lead us to love others more deeply then there is something seriously wrong with our doctrine. Doctrine was never meant to divide Christians it was supposed to spur us on to acts of love and humility. Our understanding of the scripture is to teach us to live as Christ did, loving God and loving our brother. Which Jesus explained includes those 'Samaritans' who differ from us.

Our personality is in the process of being renewed and we will all fall, but we must never excuse our sinful nature. *'The acts of the sinful nature are obvious: sexual immorality, impurity and debauchery; idolatry and witchcraft;* **hatred**, **discord**, *jealousy, fits of rage, selfish ambition,* **dissensions**, **factions** *and envy; drunkenness, orgies, and the like. I warn you, as I did before, that those who live like this will not inherit the kingdom of God. -- since we live by the Spirit, let us keep in step with the Spirit.'* Gal *5:19-21+ 25.*

Most Christians don't understand that repentance is also the way back to spiritual life. Bad attitudes to other believers, hardness of heart, inward immoral thoughts and unkind words are all serious sins. Yet instead of coming to God in confession and repentance, we justify ourselves and argue with brothers and sisters in Christ; we excuse ourselves and blame the other; we do all we can to **be right** but we don't repent and so we can never **be right with God**. *'This is what the Sovereign LORD, the Holy One of Israel, says: "In repentance and rest is your salvation, in quietness and trust is your strength, but you would have none of it.'* Isaiah 30:15.* We cannot repent of someone else's attitudes or actions, only our own, and as often as we need to, we must come back to the Cross in repentance; only then are we beginning to be renewed in the image of our creator.

A restored soul should also affect our communities since, like God; we were made to live in self-giving relationships. Once we are spiritually alive we have the potential to live as selflessly as Christ did. God's Spirit now energises our spirit, so we have the resources to draw on His strength and love as He would love. We are placed in the church for a reason. We don't just run off and find a new church when our church doesn't suit us; we build Godly loving and trusting relationships. This is hard, but the church is the means of our spiritual maturing, and the person who makes life difficult for us could well be there to help us become more like Jesus. You may have been spiritually reborn, but how is your soul, your personality developing in Christ? Are you living out the life of Jesus through your attitudes to those you meet?

'By this all men will know that you are my disciples, if you love one another." John 13:35

Finally God will **renew our bodies**; there is a foretaste of this in the healing ministry, but its fullness will come at the resurrection. *1 Cor 15:47-48 'the first man was of the earth, made of dust; the second Man is the Lord from heaven. And as we have borne the image of the man of dust, we shall also bear the image of the heavenly Man for this corruptible must put on incorruption, and this mortal must put on immortality. -- Then shall be brought to pass the saying that is written: "Death is swallowed up in victory." NKJV*

One day we will receive again a body made for eternity. God will complete his image in us, SPIRIT SOUL AND BODY. As it was in the beginning, it will be forever. Till that day, God's big plan is to renew us in the image of our creator, by the presence of the indwelling Holy Spirit as we grow in love and unity with God's people, His blood bought church.

A Prayer: May God Himself, the God of peace, sanctify you through and through. May your whole spirit, soul and body be kept blameless at the coming of our Lord Jesus Christ. The one who calls you is faithful and He will do it. The grace of the Lord Jesus Christ be with you all. 1 Thess 5:23-24

Study Questions.

1. Are you tempted to get caught up in your own little picture and miss the Big Picture of what God is doing in your life?
2. Do you agree that God still deeply loves those who are not Christians? Why is this significant?
3. What do you understand by the term 'made in the image of God'?
4. Have you any insights into the nature of God as Trinity?
5. How would you describe the Human Soul?
6. What does it mean to have knowledge of good and evil?
7. How has sin affected our Spirit - Soul - Body?
8. What is the first step in restoring the soul?
9. How do you deal with disagreements?
10. How does God want you to deal with disagreements?
11. What is God's purpose in restoring our soul?
12. How do you understand the resurrection of the dead?

For further Study: James 5 + 1Thessalonians Ch 4 & 5.

2: Repentance as the Road to Life.

*Rom 2:4, "**God's kindness leads you towards repentance.**"*

Repentance is the door to life.

Repentance was the message of John the Baptist: *Mark 1:4 "John came, baptising in the desert region and preaching a baptism of repentance for the forgiveness of sins."* As John's ministry closed and Jesus opened His ministry, He took up the same cry: *"After John was put in prison; Jesus went into Galilee, proclaiming the good news of God." The time has come," he said. "The kingdom of God is near. Repent and believe the good news!" Mark 1:14-15*

Repentance marks the start of the Christian walk.

The scripture is clear that as we repent of our sin and reach out in faith to Christ then He reaches in to us with salvation and cleansing. Yet repentance does not stop with the initial stages of the Christian walk; in order to grow in Christ it needs to be a principle constantly at work within our lives. Many Christians see repentance as something for sinners. It is true that repentance is the doorway to God's kingdom, but it is much more.

What does it mean? First let us see what it is not!

• **Repentance is not regret.** To regret something is to be sad or sorry about what has happened. There are many reasons that someone may exhibit sorrow. They may be sorry their sin was discovered, or sorry they can no longer get away with it; they may even be sorry for their own shame, but not for the hurt they have caused. There are lots of reasons to be sorry. It is good to be sorry for our sins, but sorrow and repentance are not the same. Sorrow is supposed to lead to repentance and repentance in turn leads to renewal. *2 Cor 7:10 "Godly sorrow brings repentance that leads to salvation and leaves no regret, but worldly sorrow brings death."* When we repent we don't remain in sorrow because through repentance we find forgiveness and a new start. Repentance does not just **look back** to the problem rather it **looks up** to God and **looks forward** to a new hope and a new beginning.

• **Repentance is not remorse.** Remorse is bitterness of soul. Repentance focuses on God; it is an outward and upward movement, it is a cleansing movement. Remorse is focused on the self, it looks inward and backward. It has the potential to destroy the heart and create depression and the inability to act. As it focuses on the past, it cripples the future. Remorse destroys hope. Judas was full of remorse and could only see what he had done, but not what God could do; the result was he hung himself.

- **Repentance is not reformation.** Reformation means to change our actions, to renew our character and amend our behaviour. When someone turns over a new leaf, people say: "he is a reformed man." This is part of repentance, but is not all of repentance. If we do not change our actions, we have never truly repented. However if we just changing our actions without seeking God's forgiveness and inward renewal, this is not repentance. Reform is about what we do for God; repentance is about what God does in us.

- **Repentance is not restitution.** Restitution means returning something stolen or paying its cost. It means putting right what you have done wrong. Restitution is outwards and deals with our debt to other people, but we can pay nothing to God in order to make right our debt with Him.

As a foolish youth, I once changed the price tag on an item of clothing in the shop of my employer. The dearer item was beyond my reach, but the few pounds saved meant I could afford the item. Knowing it was wrong; I paid the cheaper price and took the item home. It was only a few short months later that I became a Christian. As I learnt about repentance and restoration

God brought this theft to my mind. I was no longer working for this person but shame faced I wrote to the secretary of the company apologising and paying the money back. I was relieved to receive a letter saying they would not prosecute me for the theft.

Restoration shows if repentance has touched our heart or just affected our minds. Zaccheaus, the tax collector, as a sign of his repentance, restored four times what he had stolen (Luke 19v8-9). Restoration flows out from repentance; it is a sign of the work within but, on its own, without humility of heart, can never help us. However, if we are not willing to restore or make amends for anything we have stolen, we are not truly repentant.

An old friend of mine once came to me as a minister. He was troubled that as a young man he had been involved in armed robbery. He had prayed and sought forgiveness but still felt the guilt of his crime. My counsel was to put aside a little of his wage each week till he could repay at least the amount he had stolen and then give it back, anonymously if necessary. This he was absolutely unwilling to do. I understood the many reasons he brought up that made this difficult, but in order to be free he needed to show his repentance by an act of restoration.

How then should we define repentance? All these things are human responses to our sins, but repentance is the work of the

Holy Spirit. Repentance is a gift from God, *"God's kindness leads you towards repentance."* Rom 2:4. The Jewish Christian believers were at first amazed that *"God* had *granted even the Gentiles repentance unto life."* Acts 11:18.

Repentance is: **a change of mind** and **a change of direction**; it means seeing our lives from God's perspective; it is not just an emotional attitude of the heart. It is a decision made by **our will**; it is **a conviction** born in our hearts by the **Holy Spirit** that God is right and we are wrong. In repenting we confess our sin, knowing it is wrong; we change our attitude to sin, turn and walk away from it. If we are fully repentant we see sin as ugly, crippling and deadly. It is no longer something we wish we could do, rather we have decided is wrong; it is something that offends the holiness of God and offends our conscience. Repentance means changing our attitudes and changing our actions. It is the doorway into God's presence. When we repent **we judge our own sins** so that God will not have to judge us.

We cannot come to God without repenting. That would be like coming to God and saying: "I have done nothing wrong, I don't need to change". If we are unrepentant we have had no change of heart and no change of mind. (When I was first converted, it took me about 2 ½ years to learn the early lessons of repentance, I loved God but was still attracted by the old sins. I thank God His kindness and patience leads us to repentance.)

Repentance is foundational to our Christian life; the Bible calls it an elementary teaching: *Heb 6:1 "Therefore let us leave the **elementary teachings** about Christ and go on to maturity, not laying again the foundation of **repentance** from acts that lead to death, **and of faith** in God."*

- **Repentance is the way back to God.**

Not only is repentance the initial way to God but it also **the way back to God**, when sin tempts and seduces us again. Repentance is for Christians. The aim of repentance is not to say we are sorry, it is to restore our relationship with God. The work of the Holy Spirit is to convict us of sin and draw us back into God's loving presence. Sin will always separate us from the presence of God, and repentance is the road we walk to return to Him. For someone sensitive to God's presence many things will be seen as sin which others do not even care about. A bad temper, sarcasm, criticism and belittling others, disrespect, selfishness, insisting on our own way, impatience, lust, selfishness and pride: these are inward sins which make us unclean. If we stand unclean before God, the work of the Holy Spirit is to convict the Christian's conscience so that we can

29

return to the place of blessing. If we harden our hearts against His presence we can never find blessing. Working harder for God, reading the Bible more, praying more and witnessing are all valuable disciplines, but if we need to repent, they will not bring us back to God. The road to God is through humility and repentance.

The attitude of heart that quickly turns to God in humble repentant faith should continually be part of our Christian walk. The moment we sense the Holy Spirit convicting us of some action or attitude that offends the heart of God is the moment we should humbly bow our hearts before Him and seek His forgiveness.

- **So how do we walk in repentance?**

God has not made it difficult for the humble heart to find His blessing again. The Scripture gives a three-fold prescription to the penitent heart; it says: **remember, repent and return.**
*Rev 2:1-5 "To the angel of the church in Ephesus write: --- I know your **deeds**, your **hard work** and your **perseverance**. I know that you cannot tolerate wicked men, that you have **tested** those who claim to be apostles but are not, and have found them false. You have **persevered** and have endured hardships for my name, and have not grown weary. Yet I hold this against you: You have*

forsaken your first love. **Remember** *the height from which you have fallen!* **Repent** *and* **do the things you did** *at first. If you do not repent, I will come to you and remove your lamp stand."*

What is our first love? In my experience this is a two-fold love: it is love for God and for our brothers and sisters in Christ. A young believer instinctively loves God's people; it is only as we see their faults and receive their wounds that our love grows cold. Those who lose their first love are cold in their love for God and for His people. They have **lost their love for each other;** in this area of love, we so often sin. Yet the church is a family, and like any family they need to know that we are committed to putting things right; we are not walking out on God's family simply because we have some problems adjusting.

It begins with brokenness. We need to be willing to allow God to show us the things that are wrong in our heart. Roy Hession in his classic book on personal revival, 'The Calvary Road', focuses on sins that begin with self. "It is always self who gets irritable, envious, resentful, critical and worried. It is self who is hard and unyielding in its attitude to others. It is self who is shy, self-conscious and reserved. No wonder we need breaking. As long as self is in control, God can do little with us, for the fruit of the Spirit (see Galatians 5), with which God longs to fill us, is the complete opposite of the hard, unbroken spirit within us and presupposes that self has been crucified.

31

Being broken is both God's work, and ours. He brings His pressure to bear, but we have to make the choice. If we are really open to conviction as we seek fellowship with God, He will show us the expressions of this proud, hard self that cause Him pain. At this point we can either stiffen our necks and refuse to repent, or we can bow our heads and say, 'Yes, Lord.' Brokenness in daily experience is simply a humble response to the conviction of God." (Calvary Road p12)

"Anything that springs from self, however small, is sin. Self-effort or self-complacency in service is sin. Self-pity in trials or difficulties, self-seeking in business or Christian work, self-indulgence in one's spare time; all these are sin. Sensitiveness, touchiness, resentment, and self-defense when we are hurt or injured by others, self-consciousness, reserve, worry, fear, all spring from self." (Calvary Road p20) They make us unclean within and God calls us to renounce and repent of these attitudes.

David had it right when he said: **Ps 51:16-17** *"You do not delight in sacrifice, or I would bring it; you do not take pleasure in burnt offerings. The sacrifices of God are a broken spirit; a broken and contrite heart, O God, you will not despise."* We must come to God in humility trusting in Him to forgive and not make any excuses.

- **We must be willing to return to the Cross.** The Cross is the only place sins are dealt with. God's remedy for sin is so simple. We find it pictured in *Isaiah 35:8-9 "And a highway will be there; it will be called **the Way of Holiness**. **The unclean will not journey on** it; it will be for those who walk in that Way; wicked fools will not go about on it. **No lion** will be there, nor will any ferocious beast get up on it; they will not be found there. But **only the redeemed** will walk there."*

The picture we need to hold in mind is of mount Calvary, with the Cross standing gaunt and bloody at its summit. The mount is not high but its path is steep; there is no way to approach it but on hands and knees. As we approach the Cross bowed under sin, we see as it were a door standing open at its foot. It is a small door; only the humble may pass, and above the door is written: "By His stripes you are healed". We enter with fear, in deep humility, knowing the cost to the One Who suffered there for us. As we enter in trembling we are touched by the blood; the sacrifice is applied to our needs and we stand on the far side of the Cross blood stained, but cleansed and radiant.

The Saviour, Who had before been hanging in the agony of death, now stands beside us in glorious life; He offers His hand and we set off together along a narrow road. The road is steep but is clearly marked. It is called the Highway of Holiness and the wicked cannot go up on it, nor can anything destroy us as we walk close by Christ. The way of holiness is the way of the Cross.

When we first come to faith in Christ, we enter through the Cross. As we walk on from the Cross we become aware that others are walking the road too. Some are ahead of us beckoning us on, others are coming in behind us, and we seek to encourage them.

The road itself is built up from the surrounding landscape and runs on top of a small dyke. It is bathed in light yet the surrounding countryside is in mist and gloom. For some time we walk in joy as we travel with Christ and His people.

Then one day we are caught out, our foot slips, we sin. It may be some attitude we hold in our heart to another believer, it may be some word we have spoken or some habit that has returned to test our resolve, but as sin steps in we slip off the path. We find ourselves away from Christ and out of blessing, our joy is gone and the delight in the company of other Christians is gone. What are we to do?

The obvious thing is to get back on the road as soon as we can, but how? If we try to apply ourselves to the disciplines of the Christian life such as Bible study, witnessing to our faith or working for the Lord, we will not find again that peace of soul that comes to the forgiven heart. If we try harder to do good works and not to fall next time we will remain in self condemnation. The only way back to the road is the way of the Cross. The way we entered the road was through humility and repentance, the way we return to the road is through humility and repentance. As we begin again to admit our sin, to confess our wrong attitudes and actions and to seek Christ's forgiveness, a hand reaches into our darkness: it is the blood stained hand of Christ. He lifts us; the blood of the covenant cleanses us once more and we again walk in the light of His presence, with the joy of forgiveness in our soul.

We must learn that if the initial way to walking with Christ is through repentance and faith, then the only way to return to Christ is also through repentance and faith. This is a principle of life that we must learn to walk in. Whenever sin enters the soul and the Holy Spirit convict us of our words, attitudes or actions, we must in humility return to the Cross, confessing our faults and seeking forgiveness and a renewed walk with our Saviour. The Highway of Holiness is not a place of great striving and impossible spiritual feats of courage and discipline. It is the way of walking so closely with the Holy Spirit, that His holiness immediately convicts us when something unholy comes into our heart. In that moment we face the choice, walk in the flesh or walk in the Spirit. The two-fold work of the Holy Spirit here is to convict and to comfort; He convicts the hard-hearted and comforts the repentant.

This means agreeing with, rather than arguing with, God and being **open to conviction of sin.** *John 16:8* "*When he comes, he will convict the world of guilt in regard to sin and righteousness and judgment.*" Since the Holy Spirit is now once more living in the Human spirit, He is seeking to cleanse and direct our lives. This is the ministry of the Holy Spirit. There are several indications of His conviction; we can know a loss of peace within. If we find ourselves mentally arguing our case and trying to justify ourselves, this can be a sign that we are resisting the Holy Spirit. Anger rising against other believers is a sure sign that we are walking in the flesh and not in the Spirit. Lethargy in prayer and reluctance in Bible reading can be signs that something is spiritually wrong. A constant criticism of worship rather that enjoying God's presence betrays that we have moved from the place of blessing. The Holy Spirit never convicts us to condemn us but always to bring us back to The Cross, so that the lukewarm can become hot and the wounded receive God's peace. *"Brothers, stop thinking like children. In regard to evil be infants, but in your thinking be adults."* *1 Cor 14:20*

• I remember once seeking to explain, the principle of walking with the Holy Spirit and returning to the Cross, to a lady who was struggling with her faith. Her reply was: "I can't go round always looking for my sins that would make me miserable." NO! The truth was it would make her clean! She assumed we must look for our sins; I find that my sins are looking for me and that the Holy Spirit brings to mind when I need to come in repentance. If I lose the sense of God's peace within that is a sure sign that I have grieved the Holy Spirit. The Spirit has not left me, He simply comes to convict and restore; God's aim is always restored fellowship. The only thing that can hold is back is a hard heart.

- We need to **make repentance a lifestyle. Since it is** *"God's kindness* that *leads you towards repentance" Rom 2:4, we* need not fear God's welcome. It may be the first time that we have to humble ourselves and admit our sin, or it may be the one thousand and first. The Cross is still God's only remedy for sin. He longs for fellowship with us and His love is always seeking to draw us back. We can **depend on His welcome** because God's nature never changes, *"if we are faithless, he will remain faithful, for he cannot disown himself." 2 Tim 2:13.* The only time the scripture depicts God running, is when the prodigal returns. Repentance is a lifestyle. It is the means by which we enter the Christian walk and it is the means by which we return to Christ when sin again deceives us and destroys our walk with God.

Study Questions.

1. Why is repentance the door to the Christian faith?
2. Why must repentance be linked with faith?
3. How do regret, remorse, reformation and restitution differ from repentance?
4. How would you define repentance?
5. Do you know any examples of people showing their repentance by offering restitution?
6. Do we see the self as a problem?
7. Do we see repentance as the road back to life in Christ?
8. What are the three steps back to God in Rev 2:1-5?
9. What do we do instead of repenting?
10. How do humility and repentance work together?
11. How does the Holy Spirit work in bringing us to repentance?
12. What is the difference between condemnation and conviction?
13. Do we need to repent of our attitudes to other Christians?
14. How will we show our repentance is real?

Further readings: Psalm 51 & 32, Isaiah 35, Hebrews 6:1-3.

A prayer: Father whenever my heart is hard, draw me quickly to the cross. May the suffering of Jesus never seem small to me; bring me in worship through the door of repentance into new life. Amen.

3: The Search for Significance.

Each one of us has a deep-seated need to find meaning in our lives. As we become older we can settle for less or seek to become wiser. King Solomon faced the same dilemma. He says, *'I wanted to see what was worth while for men to do under heaven during the few days of their lives.' Eccl 2:3. 'Yet when I surveyed all that my hands had done and what I had toiled to achieve, everything was meaningless, a chasing after the wind; nothing was gained under the sun.' Eccl 2:11*

One of the reasons I wrote this book is that this year I turned fifty. And I wanted to see 'what was worthwhile for a man to do in the few days of his life on earth.' The seven ages of man have been described as spills, drills, thrills, bills, ills, pills and wills. I realise that my strength and vigour are not what they once were. Older people laugh and dismiss the aches and pains as insignificant, if only they were fifty again. Someone said: if you can still do the things at 50 that you were doing at 20, you weren't doing much at 20. The grey hairs are there, the waistline too. Policemen look like children, children have become teachers and I have finally made a will. After two years of squinting, I gave way to glasses but I am still resisting the hearing aid for my damaged ear. I ache when I ride my motorcycle and look forward to a good night in. This is not a rant or a complaint; I just realise there are far fewer days in front than behind me, and I really want to make them count for God. My philosophy has always been: if you are knocked down, seek God, stand up, work harder, and run faster. It seemed to work at 30+ but now it just exhausts me. Am I any wiser now that I am 50? Am I any closer to God? Cassius Clay said: 'the man who views the world at 50 the same as he did at 20 has wasted 30 years of his life.' The real question is: "can I, and can you, become someone who is genuinely close to God? Will we spend our years in declining futility, or will we truly sing 'what a friend we have in Jesus?'"

Looking in all the wrong places.
The problem with so many people is that they look in the wrong place for lasting happiness and significance. We assume that we will find fulfilment in money or status; we pursue possessions and end up with a house full of what? People look for pleasure in holidays, sex and hobbies. I recently came across a new phrase, the 'flirty fifties.' Some people realising their strength is waning, turn to an affair in their 50s as a way to regain their youth. Other people try to leave something for posterity. Absalom, King Solomon's brother, built his tower, hoping his name would be remembered after he died. *'Absalom had taken a pillar and erected it in the King's Valley as a monument to himself, for he*

thought, *"I have no son to carry on the memory of my name." 2 Sam 18:18.* We would all like to leave a monument and to have our names remembered. This desire for significance is deeply rooted in our personality and to understand it we need to go back to our **three part make up**: the fact that we are **spiritual** and **emotional** as well as **physical** beings. If we look to fulfil our desire for significance in any of the things we have mentioned, we will always fail, because these are unable to satisfy the soul. The Scripture calls them broken cisterns. *Jeremiah 2:13 'My people have committed two evils; they have forsaken me the fountain of living waters, and hewed them out cisterns, broken cisterns, that can hold no water.' KJV.* A broken cistern is of no use, it holds no water.

A Special Creation.

So far we have just begun to understand that people are unique in their internal make up. We are the only **tripartite beings**, consisting of Body, Soul, and Spirit, made in the image of God. We saw in chapter one, that because we were made to bear the Creator's image, that we are moral and relational beings. God was clear about this when He said of Adam, *'It is not good that the man should be alone; I will make him an help meet for him. Gen 2:18. KJV.*

God has always existed in a perfectly selfless relationship. Between the members of the Trinity, there has never been any hint of disagreement. The Father perfectly loves and relates to the Son, the Son fully loves and expresses the Father's wisdom and desires. The Son exists in and is loved by the Holy Spirit and the Holy Spirit perfectly expresses the love of the Father and Son to us. Because God is a selfless loving being in a perfect relationship, we are made to love selflessly and live in committed loving relationships. We understand this as we get older, because we find that our joys do not come though experiences, but our deepest joys come through our relationships.

We also learn form the Scriptures that God is a thinking, feeling and emotional being. This is a side of the character of God that has been largely lost to theology.

- God loves: Jeremiah 31v3, 1Jn4:8.
- God has compassion: Ps 103:13, Matt 20:34.
- God cherishes His people: Psalm 17:14 + 83:3.
- God laughs at the wicked: Ps2:4 + 59:8.
- God is jealous of our affection: Ex20:5, Josh 24:19.
- His mind is immense: Psalm 92:5, Rom 11:34.
- God is abundantly creative: Gen 1:27, Eph 2:10.

These are just some of the characteristics of the heart of God. Since God is a thinking, feeling, loving, rational and creative being then, we, who are made in His image, are also created as thinking, feeling, loving, rational and creative beings. Our emotional make up, though fallen, is a mirror of the heart of God. The mirror is shattered, but we may still gain glimpses of the heart of God in the soul of man.

Though we have three distinct parts to our being, they are in no way separate. What happens to the Body affects the Soul, as what happens in the Spirit affects the Soul. The Soul, our mind emotions and personality, are the exchange point between both the physical life and spiritual life. This means that our health can have an affect our spiritual life and our emotional condition can affect our spiritual condition.

A damaged Soul.
Since Adam was made primarily to live in a relationship with God and we have lost that relationship, it becomes obvious that to find spiritual life, we need our relationship with God to be restored.

Adam and Eve drew their emotional wellbeing directly from God Himself. Their relationship with God provided the foundation for their personality. As the Holy Spirit dwelt within their human spirits, they felt a sense of security, worth and significance.

43

Each of us, at the core of our personality, carries these three needs. We need to feel **secure** and this sense of security comes through being unconditionally loved. We need to feel a sense of **self worth** and we feel our worth when we know that we are valued. We need to feel our lives are **significant** and significance comes through realising our life has purpose and meaning. In the original creation the first human couple drew their security, self-worth and significance from God. They knew they **were loved**, since the Creator dwelt in and walked with them. They knew they **were valued** because, as the pinnacle of God's creation, they were the only ones God could commune with. They understood **their significance** as they stepped forward under God's hand to rule His creation. God said to Adam, *"Rule over the fish of the sea and the birds of the air and over every living creature that moves on the ground." Gen 1:28.*

Now that we are separated from God through sin and His Spirit no longer dwells within our spirit, we find that our psychological make up is profoundly affected. We have the same need to be loved, valued and find purpose in life but we no longer find this need met in God. Indeed we no longer have the ability or desire to draw our emotional wellbeing from God. Each of us at some time struggles with insecurity, the sense of worthlessness and insignificance.

Because we were created in God's image the creator instilled within us the **freedom of choice**. Adam's freedom of choice was tested; he was free to obey or disobey the command of God. This test is depicted in the account of the fall from Grace. *Gen 2:16-17 "The LORD God commanded the man, saying, of every tree of the garden you may freely eat: But of the tree of the knowledge of good and evil, you shall not eat of it: for in the day that you eat thereof you shall surely die." KJV.* Adam had total freedom to choose to obey or disobey this prohibition. He had the freedom to choose his actions, but he did not have the freedom to choose the consequences of his actions; and the consequences were devastating to his personality.

Instead of love, he felt guilt and shame (he knew he was naked and covered himself Gen 3:7). Instead of worth, he felt fear and anxiety (he heard the sound of God walking in the garden and hid from His presence Gen 3:10). Instead of significance, he felt anger and resentment (Adam blamed his wife and Eve too tried to pass on the blame Gen 3:12). The mind, emotions and personality of the human race were profoundly affected. A foolish choice led to fatal consequences. Death had entered into the soul of man and has affected each part of our make up. As thinking, feeling, loving, rational and creative beings we now experienced both good and evil. Guilt and shame, fear and anxiety, anger and bitterness became part of our psychological make up. God the Holy Spirit could no longer abide in an unholy residence. This is the current condition of the soul without Christ, the RUACH or breath of God has left and we look to other areas to fulfil our longings. Our soul that was made for greatness has been invaded by petty selfishness and fear in our thoughts and our actions. This affects all our relationships, at home, in the family, in the wider community and at our work.

Yet though the human soul is wounded, it retains the same basic needs; each of us still needs to feel security through being loved, worth through being valued and significance through finding the purpose for our lives. If we could place a stethoscope on the human soul and translate the cry at the core of our being into words it would be saying: 'I need to be loved, won't someone please show me love?' As Freddie Mercury said: 'can anybody find me somebody to love?'

The broken cisterns we turn to in order to fulfil our needs, such as wrong relationships, achievements, hobbies and work, can never fully satisfy the inner cry of the soul. Not all man's desires are wrong. Diligence in work, a good marriage and needed times of rest and refreshment are all part of God's gifts in our lives, but unless we address the needs of the soul, we will never find contentment within. Simply addressing outward concerns cannot meet the needs of our soul.

He restores my soul.

God's answer it to restore the soul. This process has three stages. We are made spiritually alive through the new birth: John 3:3-7. God then takes up residence within our Spirit once more and seeks to renew us in the image of our Creator. (We will look at these a little more in the next chapter.) He will finally restore us to His presence at the resurrection.

Once we are spiritually alive, the question for us is: " where do we draw our spiritual strength from? Do we draw from the polluted streams of the world or do we learn to draw our security, self-worth and significance from God directly?"

God is seeking to fill us with His love so that we will become emotionally fulfilled people and rather than looking to meet our needs elsewhere, we will draw our strength from Him. In drawing our strength from God, we will then have reserves from which to minister to others. It is as we draw strength from God that we find the energy to look outwards and meet others' needs.

God heals us from the inside out; His Spirit indwells our spirit telling us we are loved. *Rom 8:16 'The Spirit himself testifies with*

47

our spirit that we are God's children' and God deeply loves his children. Then the love of the Spirit floods into our soul, affecting our personality, and we are 'transformed by the renewing of our mind.' Rom 12:2 NKJV. This transformation deepens as we continue to draw on the strength and presence of God. (2Cor 3:18.) The process of restoring the soul is not the work of a moment it is the work of God's Spirit and God's Word over a life time.

How we learn to draw strength from the presence of God is the art of Christian living.

If we are determined to draw inward strength form God then there are certain disciplines we need to put in place. The Christian life may be more of an art than a science, but it is an art that must be practiced diligently. We are not called to be occasional visitors in God's presence but to live in His presence, being daily renewed by the Spirit of Grace.

In closing this chapter I want to look at some of the **basic steps to Spiritual health.**

Four steps to spiritual health are found in the first Christian sermon on the day of Pentecost. Acts 2:42, 'They continued *steadfastly in the **apostles' doctrine** and **fellowship**, and in* **breaking of bread**, *and in* **prayers**.' KJV

The teachings / doctrines of the Apostles have been preserved for us in the New Testament. Just as the early church was committed to learning from the Apostles, so we must commit ourselves to learn from the Scriptures. The authors of the New Testament were eye witnesses of Jesus' life. Peter makes this clear: *2 Peter 1:16 'We did not follow cleverly invented stories when we told you about the power and coming of our Lord Jesus Christ, but we were eye-witnesses of his majesty.'* We may trust the accounts of the Apostles. However we do not read merely to gain knowledge; we read to teach our soul the ways of God. It is the living and active word of God that inspires, guides and instructs our soul, and the soul is far bigger than the mind. If we are a believer who leaves their Bible unread, we are impoverishing our own soul.

Sunday by Sunday preachers prayerfully ascend the pulpit steps to hold out the word of life. Under the hand of God's Holy Spirit they offer us living bread. When a preacher steadily burns with the glow of heaven, we get a glimpse of the heart of God. We may not have the Apostles today but we do have preachers and ministers who are *'diligent to present* themselves *approved to*

God as a workman who does not need to be ashamed, accurately handling the word of truth.' 2 Tim 2:15 NASU

Fellowship: There is no such thing as a solitary Christian. We are called to be joined in common cause with God's people. We fellowship with God and with each other when we worship God together and when we join in small groups to encourage each other and draw close to God. When we follow Christ, He calls us to be part of His church. If we are not part of a small group in addition to Sunday worship, we will struggle to grow in Christ.

Breaking of bread: This phrase has two meanings. On the simple level, this shows us that the early church often ate together. As the great success of the ALPHA course has shown, there is still much benefit in eating together as Christians. Our homes are to be places of welcome and encouragement. Most of the early Christian places of worship were in homes, so sharing meals was commonplace for the early church. However the phrase 'breaking of bread' came to have a deeper significance to believers. This referred to the communion meal they shared, when they obeyed Jesus in taking bread and wine and shared together in remembering His death for their sins. Communion is not an option for believers, it is a command. Jesus said, *'Take, eat: this is my body, which is broken for you: this do in remembrance of me.' 1 Cor 11:24 KJV* If we do not take the

Lord's supper or communion, we are disobeying Christ's direct command and disrespecting His sacrifice. Communion is the place of spiritual fellowship with God and with His people, it is vitally important.

Prayer: Prayer in its essence is talking to God; the early church prayed about everything and found God answering their prayers. Though we should bring our needs to God, we should also think of the true purpose of prayer as entering into God's presence. We need to rethink prayer as a love encounter, and learn to walk with God as the lover of our soul. Worship, silence, music and meditation on God's Word all have a part in our prayer life.

These are the basic steps that many Christians will be familiar with; if we are diligent in these we will begin to grow. In the next chapter, we need to develop our understanding of God's work in restoring the soul and see what we may do to deepen our walk with Him.

A prayer: Lord, teach me to pray. Let my times in your presence become joyful and rich. Show me your glory in Jesus' name. Amen.

Study Questions.

1. Have we ever felt that life was meaningless?
2. If the book of life had 8 chapters, which would you be on?
3. What is a broken cistern?
4. What are some of the wrong places people look in for life?
5. Have you looked in any of these and are you still looking at them?
6. Does it make sense that we are made to relate selflessly?
7. Is God an emotional being?
8. How should our emotions display His presence?
9. Do we recognise our need to be loved valued and significant?
10. Do we recognise in ourselves the negative emotions of guilt and shame, fear and anxiety, bitterness and resentment?
11. 'We are free to choose, but we cannot choose the consequences of our choice.' Discuss.
12. Are we drawing spiritual strength from God?
13. What is the difference between the Soul and the Spirit?
14. What are the four basic steps of Christian growth?
15. Are you missing out any of the four key steps to growth?

Further reading: Ecclesiastes 12, 1Corinthians 11: 17 – 34.

4: Justified –Sanctified– Glorified.

If we are to develop a meaningful walk with Christ, we must learn to walk with the Holy Spirit. Paul tells us, *'Walk in the Spirit, and you shall not fulfil the lust of the flesh.' Gal 5:16. KJV.*

Jesus promises His follower's abundant life. He says: *'I am come that they might have life, and that they might have it more abundantly.' John 10:10 KJV.* Yet most of us never find this abundant life; we walk in our religious duties and miss the dance of the Spirit. We must cultivate this relationship if we are to know abundant life.

God has placed longings in our lives and they are essentially very simple. We long to be **loved,** we long to be **accepted** and we long to be **valued** as someone unique and precious. We long for a life that has some **meaning** and purpose.

As we have seen, the problem is we look in the wrong places to satisfy these longings. We think that our work, our relationships, our achievements, our love life, our hobbies, our possessions or our holidays will give us satisfaction and meaning. Many of these things are good; they can even be a gift of God, but they don't bring lasting fulfilment. **Eccl 3:11** God, *"has also set eternity in the hearts of men; yet they cannot fathom what God has done."*

The church in Corinth may be instructive to us; it is a very strange CHURCH BY OUR STANDARDS. This church was absolutely full of gross indecency and sin. They hadn't just made mistakes, they had indulged in all kinds of evil and this was sometimes after their conversion. They were looking in the wrong places to satisfy the longings in their hearts. *1 Cor 6:9-11 "Do you not know that the wicked will not inherit the kingdom of God? Do not be deceived: Neither the sexually immoral nor idolaters nor adulterers nor male prostitutes nor homosexual offenders nor thieves nor the greedy nor drunkards nor slanderers nor swindlers will inherit the kingdom of God. And that is what some of you were. But you **were washed**, you were **sanctified**, you **were justified** in the name of the Lord Jesus Christ and by the Spirit of our God."*

This was a church full of ex-slanderers, swindlers, prostitutes and drunkards. God had forgiven their past and changed their lives, now He was rebuilding their character. The Bible uses two specific and separate words to describe this process. The one is justified, the other is sanctified. God is in the business of rebuilding broken people, *'He restores my soul:' Ps 23:*3 said King David. Here the Scripture shows us how God restores our souls.

The first step is justification. If to beautify is to make beautiful, and to pacify is to make peaceful, so to justify is to make just. When we speak of being justified we do not mean that we were justified in taking some action or other, in theological terms this is a spiritual and legal standing before God. We are *'justified* [made just] *by faith in Christ.' Gal 2:16.* St Paul spends most of the books of Romans and Galatians explaining this principle.

The old evangelical memory aid that tells us: "Justified means: Just - as if - I'd not sinned", though helpful, is not rich enough in meaning. God justifies us when, in exchange for faith in Christ's sacrifice, He clothes us in Christ's righteousness and treats Christ as a sinner. We are clothed in His cleanness and treated as a son, while He is clothed in our filth and treated as an enemy of God. Through faith, in the blood-stained Cross, what Christ was, we become and what we were, Christ becomes.

We need to be absolutely clear about this. In order for us to be justified before God Jesus bears our sins. *2 Cor 5:21 "He made Him who knew no sin to be sin for us, that we might become the righteousness of God in Him." NKJV*

The depth of the sorrow that Jesus took upon Himself when He bore our sin is a mystery; we cannot fully comprehend today. We see something of His sorrow in Gethsemane, as He weeps drops of blood. I believe He does not for fear of the Cross but is repulsed at the thought of bearing human sin within His sinless soul.

We can only begin to grasp the horror of this to Jesus when we realise how vile He really felt sin was. Unlike us, He was never tempted by sin. We find sin attractive; this is its temptation, our flesh is attracted to it and we desire the brief but pleasurable experience sin provides. We are enticed by sin. James makes this clear in his letter. *James 1:14 'each man is tempted, when he is drawn away by his own lust, and enticed. ASV.* We should not be surprised that sin is attractive to us since we are fallen beings. Sin is not an outward action; it is an inward principle, deeply woven into our personality. Basically we sin because we want to sin. Until God's Holy Spirit again lives in our human spirit, we have not strength to defeat the inward pollution of sin.

The difference with Jesus is that He was not a fallen being; He was born by the power of the Spirit of God resting upon Mary. The Holy Spirit was part of His DNA from His conception. The Bible is clear *'knew no sin' 2 or 5:21.* Sin never enticed or attracted Jesus, even for a millisecond. He found it repulsive, and His pure nature recoiled in horror from its ugliness. We cannot state this strongly enough: this is the mystery of the

Cross, the one who was utterly repelled and nauseated by sin, became sin for us. The utter devastation He experienced, as sin entered His undefiled soul, cannot be imagined. No wonder we worship Him, how could we not worship Him? *'He himself bore our sins in his body on the tree, that we might die to sin and live to righteousness. By his wounds you have been healed. 1 Peter 2:24 RSV*

The wonder of the sinless one bearing our sins is only the first half of justification. Next as we place our faith in His atoning sacrifice, He applies forgiveness to us. In doing this He not only forgives our past, but also our present and future sins.

This was brought home to me as I read Max Lucado recently. In his book, 'The Eye of the Storm', Max comments of Jesus healing miracles and speculates that as He heals the sick, Jesus also knows the hearts of the people He is healing. John tells us, *'He did not need man's testimony about man, for he knew what was in a man.' John 2:25.* Undoubtedly there were people among the crowd who would use their new found health for evil purposes. Since Christ could see into men's souls, was He tempted to say to the rapist or the bigot: "I can never heal you"? As He healed a man who was unable to speak, He would know if that man would use his tongue to blaspheme and lie. As He healed the withered hand, He knew if that man would beat his wife. Yet even with this ability to see into the soul, He never once refuses to heal.

As I read I found myself looking down the history of my own life. I became a Christian at nineteen years of age. My teenage years had been far from spotless, but I knew that Christ had forgiven my past. What I realized at that moment was that when Christ accepted me, He not only saw my past sins, He saw my future sins as well. He saw all that I would do at twenty-three and thirty-seven and at fifty. He did not say: "I cannot forgive or accept you because of your future sins." His grace saw me, knew me fully and yet forgave and received me. *'He forgave us all our sins, having cancelled the written code, with its regulations, that was against us and that stood opposed to us; he took it away, nailing it to the Cross.' Col 2:13-14.* This thought is deeply humbling: Christ's love has covered the multitude of our sins, yours and mine, past, present and future.

To be justified involves Christ bearing my penalty and me accepting His forgiveness. It is for us to be granted the legal standing of a son of God, whilst God, the Son takes the punishment of the outcast. When we are justified God treats us as if we are Jesus and treats Jesus as if He was us. This brings us into a new relationship of peace with God. *"Since we have been justified through faith, we have peace with God through our Lord Jesus Christ." Rom 5:1.*

We must never think God does not love us; the depths of His love for us correspond exactly to the depths of His punishment of Jesus. Since He was treated as the vilest of sinners, we will be treated as the dearest of sons. We are treated as true sons and daughters of God; while the Son of God is treated as a despised sinner.

To be justified is the first step in remaking our lives; the second step is to be **sanctified.** The first step happens in a moment; the second is the work of a lifetime. Through God's work within, we start to become the children that God called us to be.

In 1955, the Queen commissioned two portraits: one by the Italian artist Annigoni, the other by the Canadian photographer Karsh. The photographer set the light and positioned Her Majesty to make the most of her natural beauty. In a short time, the picture was taken and the image indelibly captured. This is justification: in a moment, we are clothed in royal robes, and the image of Christ is impressed on our soul. Annigoni, on the other hand, had several sittings with Her Majesty. He studied in detail her appearance and slowly built up the painting in oils from his palette. Eventually after much painstaking work, the royal image emerged. This is sanctification: God taking His palette and slowly painting His image on our soul, until we emerge as a child who bears the likeness of the King.

God's work in us is to remould, rebuild, remake and reform. He is developing the very character of Jesus within us, as a son of God must resemble the Son of God.

To be sanctified actually means: to be set aside for Holy use. Once God has cleansed the vessel, it is fit for His use. You *are not your own? For you are bought with a price: therefore glorify God in your body, and in your spirit, which are God's.' 1Cor 6:19-20. KJV m.*

God's ownership shows in our attitude to sin, as illustrated at Corinth. *"Do not be deceived: Neither the sexually immoral nor idolaters nor adulterers nor male prostitutes nor homosexual offenders nor thieves nor the greedy nor drunkards nor slanderers nor swindlers will inherit the kingdom of God. And that is what some of you were." 1Cor 6:9-11.* At the very outset of his letter, Paul identifies their need; they are set aside for God's use (sanctified) and called to be Holy. *'To the church of God in Corinth, to those sanctified in Christ Jesus and called to be holy.' 1 Cor 1:2*

God does not leave us the same as He finds us. He is beginning to prepare us for eternity, so that we do not only live, but thrive in the presence of His Holiness.

The Apostle John assures us that: *"No-one who is born of God will continue to sin, because God's seed remains in him; he cannot go on sinning, because he has been born of God."* *1John 3:9.* Before we come to faith in Christ, sin attracts us; now we begin to share Christ's attitude as we see its true ugliness. We no longer excuse our sin but we mourn our sin. Theodore Monod expresses this growth in grace in his hymn:

O the bitter shame and sorrow,
That a time could ever be,
When I let the Saviour's pity
Plead in vain, and proudly answered,
"All of self, and none of Thee!"

Yet He found me; I beheld Him
Bleeding on the accursèd tree,
Heard Him pray, "Forgive them, Father!"
And my wistful heart said faintly,
"Some of self, and some of Thee!"

Day by day His tender mercy,
Healing, helping, full and free,
Sweet and strong, and ah! So patient,
Brought me lower, while I whispered,
"Less of self, and more of Thee!"

Higher than the highest heavens,
Deeper than the deepest sea,
Lord, Thy love at last hath conquered:
Grant me now my supplication,
"None of self, and all of Thee!"

This change of heart is brought about by the direct intervention of God, for in the moment we reach out in saving faith, He reaches out and plants the very seed of His nature within the human soul. This is what John expresses in 1Jn 3:9. God breathes upon us once again (Gen 2:7) and the breath of life dwells in the Human heart. Our spirit becomes the cradle of the divine Spirit. We are for the first time in our existence that which we were intended to be: a living spirit indwelt by the Holy Spirit of God.

This is why the Scripture tells us *'be transformed by the renewing of your mind.'* Rom 12:2 NKJV. For the first time, as believers, we are enabled to think and feel as God thinks and feels. His Spirit is now guiding our spirit through His word.

This process is described as a battle, the Flesh Vs the Spirit. *Gal 5:17-18 "The flesh sets its desire against the Spirit, and the Spirit against the flesh; for these are in opposition to one another, so that you may not do the things that you please."* NAS. The art of the Christian life is to learn to walk in the Spirit. If we do as we please, we will follow the lusts of the flesh; if we follow the Spirit we are set aside for God's use.

This then is how God brings us into **abundant life**; it is through re-making us and guiding us until we have learned to walk as a confidant of the Holy Spirit. God fulfils our deepest longings to be loved, valued and considered of worth, by taking up residence at the core of our being.

We know well that we cannot walk hand in hand with someone we have fallen out with. When a husband and wife are at odds, they may even walk on opposite sides of the road. God forgives and cleanses us in order to walk with us as a friend. Our deepest longings to be loved and accepted are not fulfilled by a religion; they are fulfilled by a relationship. It is this relationship with God that brings a sense of love and acceptance into our human souls.

Today many Christians are only dimly aware that this heart to heart relationship is what God is seeking to draw us into. They are actually suspicious of, or fearful of, an intimate relationship with God. We need a Spirit to spirit relationship with God Himself. *"No eye has seen, no ear has heard, no mind has conceived what God has prepared for those who love him"-- but God has revealed it to us by his Spirit. The Spirit searches all things, even the deep things of God." 1 Cor 2:9-10*

A picture in the Old Testament helps us. Moses, when he returned from Sinai, is depicted as literally radiant or glowing with the presence of God. So much so that a veil was placed over his face to hide the glory from those who saw him. Only in God's presence did he remove the veil. Now as believers we are told to remove the veil and allow God's glory to shine deeply into our lives as we behold, contemplate and reflect God's presence. *2 Cor 3:18 'But we all, with unveiled face beholding as in a mirror the glory of the Lord, are transformed into the same image from glory to glory, even as from the Lord the Spirit.' ASV*

This changed heart and life does not happen in a moment. We are forgiven in a moment through Calvary but we are changed over a life time. This is the work of sanctification that Jesus is doing in us. This is a partnership and it is our choice to cooperate with God the Holy Spirit in restoring our souls. We should all be in the process of growing in God. Is our desire to know God deeper than last year? Are we growing in grace as we draw closer to the heart of God?

What are the ways that we can access his power?

In the Temple at Jerusalem, there were people who served in the outer court and there were the priests, who served in the inner court, the 'Holy place' of the Temple. We are called to an inner court, not an outer court ministry. *Heb 10:19-22 'Therefore, brothers, since we have confidence to enter the Most Holy Place by the blood of Jesus, --- 22 let us draw near to God.'*

If we remain in the outer courts we will see many marvellous things. The outer courts are the place of song and service. This was where the sacrifices were made and the sons of Korah led the worship. It was a place of joy and fellowship, but everything in the outer court depended on the High Priest ministering in the inner court. Before we can have any meaning full outer court ministry we must spend time in the inner court. Our lifestyle will often tell us that time with God is wasted time or needless time. God longs to walk with us as he walked with Adam in the cool of the evening. Time with God is not wasted time, it is priority time. Jesus said, *'when you pray, go into your room, and when you have shut your door, pray to your Father who is in the secret place; and your Father who sees in secret will reward you openly.' Matt 6:6-7 NKJV*

• **Enter in Worship:** Our place of prayer is to become a Holy of Holies. As we enter we should enter in worship. Wesley talked about being "lost in wonder, love and praise". Worship is so much more than singing songs, but that can be our starting point. It is good to sing our way into God's presence and allow our spirits to rise with the song. We all know the joy of waking with a song on our hearts; we need to know the joy of bringing our songs to the Lord of our souls. We may move into prayer or listening, but the aim of his worship is to rest in God's presence.

One practice in prayer that has been helpful in recent years is the practice of '**Soaking**' in God's presence. This is usually done by relaxing in the presence of the Lord, whilst playing worship music. As we rest with the Lord, we allow our sprit to rise with the music. We ask God through His Spirit to dwell in us richly and we linger in His love. This can be done sitting or lying on the floor, the aim is intimacy. It takes a little time to learn but as we invite God to dwell deeply within us, His kingdom, His priorities and His peace come to rest in us. Soaking in God's presence is the antidote to a hectic lifestyle.

This deeply and personal relationship with the Holy Spirit presupposes we are not hiding sin in our hearts. If we are, the ministry of the Spirit is to convict our conscience and bring us to confession and repentance. He is also able to guide and direct us. The Holy Spirit only wants to glorify Christ in our lives and will lead us into repentance or rejoicing as is appropriate to our needs. If we see our faith as a walk with the Holy Spirit rather than a walk to another meeting, we will begin to rejoice in the joy of His presence. [Please do not hear me say that meetings are not important, the Bible enjoins us to meet for fellowship, worship, teaching and prayer.] What I am saying is that meeting with God is the most important meeting. We must have an inner court ministry, entering into His Holy presence before we can rejoice in the outer courts.

• We also need a growing **understanding of the word of God.** The Bible tells us what God thinks about things. As we breathe in its pages we begin to think God's ways. We need to make the Bible part of our daily walk. In order to read the Bible through in one year, it would only take about 3 ½ pages per day. The maths are simple: if we look at how many pages there are in our Bible and divide the total number by 365, we will see how many pages we need to read to cover the whole of God's word in a year. There is more to understanding the Bible than reading 3 ½ pages a day. There is study and meditation on the scriptures, but if we are not regular in our Bible reading we handicap ourselves. God the Holy Spirit, the author of the book is seeking to speak to us as we read His word.

• **Listening** to God is a lost art and often we are too tuned into our own desires to hear what God is saying to us. Yet God promises if we will still our souls, we will learn to hear the still small voice of God. *Isaiah 30:21 'And thine ears shall hear a word behind thee, saying, this is the way, walk ye in it.' KJV*

If our prayer times begin to include worship, the Word and listening in addition to our regular prayers, then we will begin to sense the presence of the Holy Spirit in our Human spirits. When God speaks He will not guide our thoughts to do anything contrary to the Scriptures.

If God is to restore our soul it is through cooperation with our will.

What about the body?

We have already seen that the body, soul and spirit are intimately linked. This means that to stay spiritually fresh, we also need to take care of our bodies. If we are stiff, lethargic and often feel under the weather, we may need to take control of our physical nature. What we eat can greatly affect our bodies. As a young man this seems needless; as we age, we need to take more careful care of our eating habits. What we eat will affect our bodies and our bodies will have an effect on our emotional wellbeing, our soul. So we need to discipline ourselves to eat well and not to overeat.

We must also think of appropriate physical exercise. I was recently invited to attend an exercise class sponsored by 'Help the Aged'. One lady who attended had not been upstairs in her house for months. After a few sessions, she had strengthened her legs to such a degree that the stairs presented no problem.

An unfit body can lead to a discouraged soul. We do not need to be obsessive, but if we need exercise we should take the necessary steps. Cycling, walking, swimming and the gym can all have knock on effects on our psychological make up. Exercise must not replace our physical disciplines but it is quite possible to have extra times of prayer as we walk or cycle, as long as we don't close our eyes.

Restoring the Soul: the 'hot poker principle.' This principle tells us that as long as the poker stays in the fire, it remains hot. When it is withdrawn from the fire, it begins to cool. The same is true of our spiritual lives. Each of us will have several activities in our lives that keep our Christian lives hot. These may differ for different people, as we all have differing character and personalities. Here is a list of some of the things that keep me hot.

1.   **Reading**; I have recently read most of the books in the bibliography. I aim to read Joyce Meyer on guidance next. I need to look at people who can stretch me and have something to say; so even though I read slowly, I still read.

2.   **Study**: I have the kind of mind that likes to analyze and understand, this means that in order to stay fresh I need to study.

3.   **Ministry and music CDs**. By ministry, I mean listening to great preachers; my current favourites are John Maxwell and Ed Cole on Leadership.

4.   **Solitude**: Like King David, I draw strength from withdrawing to the side of a river. When God leads me beside still water and restores my soul, that is a good day. Ps 23v3. We need to understand that we are called to have a Sabbath rest each week and extended Sabbaths in God's presence during the year. We call this a holiday; the Scriptures call them Holy Days. The Jews of old had three compulsory festivals each year; time set aside to seek God. (See appendix on the importance of Sabbath.)

5.   Godly **Conferences**, this follows on from the idea of spiritual Sabbath breaks. Over the years I have enjoyed conferences at Cliff College, Easter People, E. C. G. Tarsus and AOG conferences, as well as times of personal retreat for prayer.

6.   Time with my **wife and family:** without their support I would fail.

7.   **Godly Friends**: We all have friends who drain us. They are highly demanding and bring a sprit of turmoil into the house. We may also have friends that exude God's peace. When they enter the room God comes with them; when they leave His presence lingers. These are the friendships to cultivate; be close to those who are close to God.

8.   **Witnessing**, sharing the love of Jesus with others is such a joy and when God opens a door I always return rejoicing.

These are just some of the things that keep me strong spiritually. Your list may differ, but you would be wise to know what empowers you and what drains you and then seek to build into your life the things that keep you spiritually hot. The most important step we can take in restoring the soul is learning to walk in the friendship and presence of the Holy Spirit.

Max Lucado has a list a little like this:
- Have a weekly walk with a child.
- Make your major decisions in a cemetery.
- Live as if God is watching.
- Don't spend next week's money this week.
- Make home the first place you succeed.
- Hear more than you say.
- God forgave you, so you forgive others.
- Stand in awe of sunsets.
- Be generous not grudging.
- Treat people like a best friend and they may become one.
- God forgave you, so forgive yourself.
- God loves you, so you must be pretty special.
- Trust God even in the dark times.

- If you blow your own trumpet, it is bound to sound flat.
- The book of our lives has limited chapters; know which one you are on.
- Don't put off important things for trivial pursuits.
- Live a life of worship.
- Keep looking forward the destination may be nearer than you think. (Adapted from Max Lucado "In the Eye of the Storm")

Get to know the things that keep you spiritually hot and do them. Whichever list you follow, make sure that your priority is getting to know God. Jesus Himself told us, *'when you pray, go into your room, close the door and pray to your Father, who is unseen. Then your Father, who sees what is done in secret, will reward you.'* Matt 6:6. When we love someone we will want to spend time with them. In order to develop a love relationship with God, we must spend time in His lovely presence. It is simple to say by harder to do. Give God priority time in your life.

- There is **a third step** in God's process of restoring our soul. *Rom 8:30, "Those he called, he also justified; those he justified, he also glorified."* First He justifies, then He sanctifies, finally He will glorify this earthly body. *1 Cor 15:47-48 'The first man was of the earth, made of dust; the second Man is the Lord from heaven. And as we have borne the image of the man of dust, we shall also bear the image of the heavenly Man for this* *corruptible must put on incorruption, and this mortal must put on immortality. -- Then shall be brought to pass the saying that is written: "Death is swallowed up in victory."*

As we are sanctified through the work of the Spirit and obedience to the word of God, one day we will come to share in the beauty of the Lord for *'when we see him we shall be like him.'* 1John 3:2. *"Listen, I tell you a mystery: We will not all sleep, but we will all be changed-- in a flash, in the twinkling of an eye, at the last trumpet. For the trumpet will sound, the dead will be raised imperishable, and we will be changed. For the perishable must clothe itself with the imperishable and the mortal with immortality."* 1 Cor 15:51-53

This is the purpose of God in our lives: to forgive our sin (Justify), to make us true sons and daughters of God bearing His likeness in this world (Sanctify) and one day to redeem our bodies (Glorify). A divine plan and it begins as we submit to Jesus and follow Him. The subject of our standing in Heaven is where we must turn to in the closing chapter.

A Prayer: FATHER I thank you that you have justified me through faith in Christ. Now by your word and through your Spirit sanctify my soul, that I may more perfectly reflect the image of my Saviour. Amen.

Study Questions.

1. How does you church receive people who have a past?
2. Do we allow people to express enthusiasm for Christ in our church?
3. What does the word "justified" mean?
4. How would Christ's sinless soul respond to bearing sin?
5. Why do you think Christ wept in Gethsemane?
6. Christ knows us fully but still accepts us. How do you react to this statement?
7. What does the word "sanctified" mean?
8. Have we begun to find sin unattractive?
9. Why do we still sin?
10. Will God reject us because of our sins?
11. Do we spend time in private worship with God?
12. Have you any hints on how to hear God's voice?
13. Have you tried soaking?
14. Do you need to take any physical exercise to defeat spiritual lethargy?
15. What are your 'hot poker' principles? Turn to page 103 and fill in your top ten.
16. What does "glorified" mean?

Further readings: Galatians Ch3, 1Corinthians Ch 15

5: The judgement seat of Christ.

2 Cor 5:10 "We must all appear before the judgement seat of Christ, that each one may receive what is due to him for the things done while in the body, whether good or bad."

Most Christians understand that there is a Hell to shun and a Heaven to gain, but few realise that believers will also be judged by Christ. If we are to live in the light of eternity we need to understand the judgement we will face, and so become mature in our understanding. Knowing we will be judged should focus our thought and instil something of the fear of God into our souls.

The Proverbs tell us that *"the fear of the LORD is the beginning of wisdom" Proverbs 9:10* and that *"the fear of the LORD leads to life." Proverbs 19:23.* The New Testament church walked *"in the fear of the Lord and in the comfort of the Holy Spirit. Acts 9:31 NKJV.* Today many Christians seek the comfort of the Holy Spirit but know little of the fear of the Lord.

We understand from Scripture that there will be two **judgements:** one is the 'Great White Throne', where those who reject Christ will be judged along with the devil and his angels of darkness. The other will occur at the resurrection of the righteous when we will all stand before the judgement seat of Christ. The one is of goats, the other of sheep (Matt 25:31-46); the one is for sin, the other for faithful service. Both judgements will be genuine judgements, our sins are not overlooked.

1.   Great white throne.

Rev 20:11-15 "Then I saw a great white throne and Him who sat on it, from whose face the earth and the heaven fled away. And there was found no place for them. And I saw the dead, small and great, standing before God, and books were opened. And another book was opened, which is the Book of Life. And the dead were judged according to their works, by the things which were written in the books. The sea gave up the dead who were in it, and Death and Hades delivered up the dead who were in them. And they were judged, each one according to his works. Then Death and Hades were cast into the lake of fire. This is the second death. And anyone not found written in the Book of Life was cast into the lake of fire." NKJV

This is a fearful judgement, there is no advocate and no court of appeal; it is irrevocable and eternal. It will also be proportional, for each will be *"judged according to his works."* This is a judgement of sin, a judgement to condemnation. Christians will not be condemned since there condemnation fell on Christ for, *"He himself bore our sins in his body on the tree, that we might die to sin and live to righteousness. By his wounds you have*

76

been healed." *1 Peter 2:24-25 RSV.* Because He has borne our sin we will never bear the penalty for sin; but because he has borne our sin He bears the right to judge us. In Christ, our sins are not simply overlooked they are looked over to the Cross. They are not forgotten, they are forgiven.

2.   The judgement seat of Christ.

There is still a judgement of believers. *"We will all stand before God's judgment seat. It is written: "'As surely as I live,' says the Lord, 'every knee will bow before me; every tongue will confess to God.'" So then, **each of us will give an account** of himself to God." Rom 14:10-12.* Here Paul is speaking to believers.

The judgement seat of Christ will be of reward and of loss, not a prize giving at a school sports day. Many, many Christians are unprepared to stand before God in Judgement. They think salvation is all there is and have not matured or grown into their reward.

The principle we need to hold in mind is the principle of **proportional reward.** That each person's reward differs in heaven is very plain in the scripture. Not every Christian will receive the same reward.

Paul puts it in a simile when he speaks of the resurrection. *1 Cor 15:41-42 "The sun has one kind of splendour, the moon another and the stars another; and star differs from star in splendour. So will it be with the resurrection of the dead."* We will not all shine with the same splendour in God's heavenly kingdom.

The disciples understood this. *"Then James and John, the sons of Zebedee, came to him."Teacher," they said, "we want you to do for us whatever we ask." "What do you want me to do for you?" he asked. They replied, "Let one of us sit at your right and the other at your left in your glory." Mark 10:35-37.* They understood that in Heaven some would take first place, near to His throne.

Jesus's parables teach this. Jesus parable of the minas shows the principle of proportional reward. *"He said: "A man of noble birth went to a distant country to have himself appointed king and then to return. So he called ten of his servants and gave them ten minas. 'Put this money to work,' he said, 'until I come back.' ---- "The first one came and said, 'Sir, your mina has earned ten more.' "'Well done, my good servant!' his master replied. 'Because you have been trustworthy in a very small matter, take charge of ten cities.' "The second came and said, 'Sir, your mina has earned five more.' "His master answered, 'You take charge of five cities.' Luke 19:12-13 + 16-19.* The teaching is clear, those who prove trustworthy in this life will be trusted with greater honour in the next. *"Whoever can be trusted with very little can also be trusted with much, and whoever is dishonest with very little will also be dishonest with much. So if you have not been trustworthy in handling worldly wealth, who will trust you with true riches?" Luke 16:10-11*

Jesus continues in this very shocking illustration as He instructs Peter, *"That servant who knows his master's will and does not get ready or does not do what his master wants will be* **beaten with many blows**. *But the one who does not know and does things deserving punishment will be* **beaten with few blows**. *From everyone who has been given much, much will be demanded; and from the one who has been entrusted with much, much more will be asked." Luke 12:47-48.* Whatever we understand by the servant being beaten with few or many blows, the clear teaching is that our reward is proportional to our service.

God does not only know our actions He knows our hearts, and this is where the change must occur if we are to receive the reward God seeks to give us. The moment we step out of the clothing of this life and into eternity, what we were on the inside will be clearly evident to every one. Our motives, our thoughts, our character, our inner secrets will be openly displayed. *"What you have said in the dark will be heard in the daylight, and what you have whispered in the ear in the inner rooms will be proclaimed from the roofs." Luke 12:3. "There is nothing hidden that will not be disclosed, and nothing concealed that will not be known or brought out into the open." Luke 8:17. "I say to you that for every idle word men may speak, they will give account of it in the Day of Judgment. For by your words you will be justified, and by your words you will be condemned." Matt 12:36-37 NKJV.* God tells us, *"then we shall know fully, even as we are fully known." 1 Cor 13:12.*

When we stand before 'The Judgement Seat of Christ' what we were in this life will be transparent. There will be reward and loss; **the reward will be just**, as it will exactly measure who we were in Christ. We will be rewarded according to our faith and our obedience. We will be satisfied with our reward because it will perfectly reflect who we are in Christ. Yet our sins will not be hidden; they will be clearly known, not to make us squirm and feel ashamed, but rather to show how wonderful God's grace and mercy are, that Christ should save sinners like us. His beauty and forgiveness will seem all the more wonderful against the dark motives and inner failures of our sin. We will not boast about what we have done, but He will celebrate what He has done in us. Our testimony will be, 'this is what I truly am, and Christ has redeemed me.'

The judgement will not just be a reward, for many there **will also be loss** for what could have been. The Scriptures clearly show this. *"No-one can lay any foundation other than the one already laid, which is Jesus Christ. If any man builds on this foundation using gold, silver, costly stones, wood, hay or straw, his work will be shown for what it is, because the Day will bring it to light. It will be revealed with fire, and the fire will test the quality of each man's work. If what he has built survives, he will receive his reward. If it is burned up, he will suffer loss; he himself will be saved, but only as one escaping through the flames."* 1 Cor 3:11-15.

Every Christian builds their life on Christ and His finished work of salvation but how we build on this foundation will be shown in our eternal standing. In Heaven we build our own house by the works we do while here. Gold, silver and precious stones are materials that are refined by fire; wood, hay and stubble are burned up in the flames. For some of us as we enter the Gates of Heaven our life work will prove to be wood, hay and straw in the sight of God.

This is our situation; there are two judgements, one for sin and one for service. If Christ has forgiven our sin, then we will not be judged to Hell, the wrath of God has fallen on Christ and we are forgiven, but we will be judged for service. For *"We must all*

appear before the judgement seat of Christ, that each one may
receive what is due to him for the things done while in the body,
whether good or bad." 2 Cor 5:10

What will we be judged for and how do we gain a reward?

Firstly we will be judged for our **obedience** to God's revealed
word. There is an old saying that comes from the puritans: 'the
law sends us to Christ for salvation, and Christ sends us back to
the law for sanctification.'   There is a grain of truth in this, but it is
not the whole truth.

We are called to walk in obedience to the **Word of God and the**
Spirit of God. There is a great danger here of religious pride. If
we manage to obey the word of God, the result is that we think
we are doing fairly well as Christians. Then we begin to judge
those who do not obey the same set of religious commands and
rules as us. We can actually begin to measure our progress by
how well we keep the commandments. What has happened?
We have moved from grace back to law.

This is the attitude of the **Pharisee.** It is rife in the Church and
shows in many ways. It shows in the superiority of one
denomination over another and open suspicion of other believers.
It shows in putting church rules before the needs of people and in

insisting that things are done by the book and according to the tradition. It binds the heart and saps the soul; it condemns the joy in others and finds no joy itself. It elevates one Bible version or hymn book to such a place that anyone who does not use it is immediately suspect and needs to be instructed in the deeper truths of God. It judges and criticises. We are called to obey God's word in the power of His Spirit. His word is not just a book of rules; it is a book of life, and its top two commandments are: "to love God and love our brothers in Christ" [Luke 10:12]. If our doctrine does not lead us to a profound love of God and His people then our doctrine is profoundly mistaken.

If we are to stand clean on judgement day we need to get beyond legalism into a relationship with God. *John 4:24 "God is Spirit, and those who worship Him must worship in spirit and truth." NKJV*

The attitude of religion is a **'can't do' attitude**, it is negative and probative. God wants a relationship with His people, not a religion. It is the **Spirit of God who enables our spirit to walk in truth.** It is not a matter of self-effort and grim determination as we keep God's commandments; it is walking so close to the Holy Spirit that we could not even think of wounding God and losing His presence. *Gal 5:25 "Since we live by the Spirit, let us keep in step with the Spirit."*

Here is the deeper truth; God is looking at our **attitudes**. *"Let this mind be in you which was also in Christ Jesus, who, being in the form of God, did not consider it robbery to be equal with God, but **made Himself of no reputation**, taking the form of a bondservant, and coming in the likeness of men. And being found in appearance as a man, **He humbled Himself.**"* Phil 2:5-8

If the Son of God was clothed in humility, we have no option but to **walk humbly** before Him. *"What does the LORD require of you? To act justly and to love mercy and to walk humbly with your God."* Mic 6:8. The first virtue a Christian must put on is **humility.** The badge of heaven on earth is not glory but humility, it is not self-centredness, it is Christ likeness. Peter tells us to *"be clothed with humility, for "God resists the proud, But gives grace to the humble." 1 Peter 5:5 NKJV*

The importance of Humility.

We need to understand the importance of **humility:** to some it implies inadequacy, a lack of dignity, or worthlessness. To be humble seems to mean: being small and despised. The world values strength and boldness, yet Jesus says, *"I am meek and lowly in heart:" Matt 11:29 KJV.* The world looks for 'pride of place' but Jesus says, *"Blessed are the meek, for they will inherit the earth. Matt 5:5.*

True humility does not mean despising ourselves, it is realising that all our strength is found in God. The Nelson's Bible Dictionary defines humility as: 'A freedom from arrogance that grows out of the recognition that all we have and are comes from God.'

Selwyn Hughes identifies three areas of true humility, **1:** It is a right estimate of ourselves. We understand that we are sinful by nature, but we also know that we are valued and loved as children of God. **2:** Self-forgetfulness; for the humble person their life does not revolve around their goals and desires, it revolves around God's goals and desires. A humble person is so taken up with Christ and seeking to be a blessing that selfish desires are burned up in His presence. **3:** The humble person recognises that without God they can do nothing. The proud person thinks God can do nothing without them.

Pride is the opposite of humility. CS Lewis said, 'There can be no surer proof of a confirmed pride, than a belief that one is sufficiently humble.'

Our template is Jesus. *'Let this mind be in you that was in Christ Jesus.'* It is His humility we are called to wear, and the cloak of humility is the mark of heaven.

How might pride show?

We can be proud that we are Christians or Anglicans, Baptists, Methodists or Pentecostals. We can be proud that we have stood where others have fallen. We can be proud of our knowledge of the Bible, our preaching or our ability to pray. We can be proud of our tradition and our history. Ordinary things can also be the cause of pride; our house, our car, our ability or our appearance can be a source of pride. Pride is not a little sin; it keeps God at a distance. When we think we are right and others are wrong, pride coupled with self-righteousness becomes very ugly indeed.

Humility shows chiefly in our attitude to other Christians, but also shows in our attitude to those who do not believe. Just before we are told to have the attitude of Christ, Paul tells us to make his *"joy complete by being like-minded, having the same love, being one in spirit and purpose. Do nothing out of selfish ambition or vain conceit, but in humility consider others better than yourselves." Phil 2:1-2.*

The smallest hint of pride in our hearts will separate us from God's blessing, because *"God opposes the proud but gives grace to the humble." Humble yourselves, therefore, under God's mighty hand, that he may lift you up in due time." 1 Peter 5:5-6.* The attitude of humility brings God's favour, *"for though the*

LORD is exalted, yet He regards the lowly, but the haughty He knows from afar." Ps 138:6 NASU

Without humility we cannot walk in the presence of the Lord; without humility all our works are wood, hay and straw; they will be burned up in the fire of Judgement. The hymn writer understood this when they wrote: "Let holy charity my outer vesture be, and lowliness become my inner clothing; true lowliness of heart, which takes the humbler part, and o'er its own shortcomings weeps with loathing." God is not looking for outward obedience to religious laws but an inward attitude of heart, which means we are beginning to think and act as Christ would think and act.

Robbers of our reward.

There are several obvious areas which will rob us of our reward.

• **The first is compromising habits.** Some sins are hard to break, they have a hold on us, and they are often related to addiction or lust. [However it can just as easily be a habit to moan and complain; a negative attitude to life and people can be a habit.] We basically sin because we enjoy it, but we do not realise our habitual sins are bringing death into our lives. *James 1:14-15 'Each one is tempted when he is drawn away by his own desires and enticed. Then, when desire has conceived, it gives birth to sin; and sin, when it is full-grown, brings forth death.'* If we **make**

87

a truce with our besetting sins then we will never know the victory Christ desires in our lives. Jesus is very clear here, He says, *"I tell you the truth, everyone who sins is a slave to sin. Now a slave has no permanent place in the family, but a son belongs to it for ever." John 8:34-35.* As sons of God we are not called to make a truce with our sins; we are called to gain the victory over our sins. Jesus did not say: "blessed are the truce makers", He said, *'blessed are the peace makers.' Mt 5:9.* We need to battle our sins till we win the victory and so have gained peace. In over 30 years of walking the Christian road I have found that the only thing that keeps me from sin is living in the presence of God. When I am too busy and God seems distant, sin is attractive; when God is close, sin is repulsive. Habits that master us must be brought to the Cross in confession and repentance so that we can find new life and strength in Christ. If we say our habits are not sinful we are only deceiving ourselves.

• **Our Relationships.** It is those we are closest to that we often hurt the most. Husbands, do you love your wife? We took a vow to love on our wedding day, but does our wife know to the depths of her soul that she is loved? We will be judged on how our relationships are lived out. If we are more interested in our work than our family, we will be judged. If our children do not know how precious they are to us, then we have missed God's best for our lives and theirs. A strong marriage relationship is the most important thing we can build on this earth. Our families are a gift from God and we must invest the time needed to show them our love and devotion. When they take second place to anything but God, we stand under the judge's scrutiny.

Our relationships do not only include our immediate family; they extend to our Christian brothers and sisters. Many of the New Testament epistles begin with doctrine but then move on to instruct Christians on how to treat each other. Corinthians speaks of division factions, court cases and immorality. Galatians, Romans and Colossians remind us that there are no longer any racial barriers between believers. *Col 3:11 'There is neither Greek nor Jew, circumcised nor uncircumcised, barbarian, Scythian, slave nor free, but Christ is all and in all.'* The most important thing is to treat each other with honour and respect. *Col 3:12 'Therefore, as God's chosen people, holy and dearly loved, clothe yourselves with compassion, kindness, humility, gentleness and patience.'*

These injunctions to live as people of the light, carrying the attitude of Christ toward each other, are the expected application of our doctrine. If we are complaining, uncooperative, critical, accusative, bad tempered and unkind to God's people then, we have disobeyed His word and God Himself will hold us to account. The Bible is very clear on this *'Don't grumble against each other, brothers, or you will be judged. The Judge is standing at the door!' James 5:9.* Our attitudes matter to God; the way we treat our family and our brothers or sisters in Christ is measured by God and He will hold us to account. *'Therefore, as we have opportunity, let us do good to all, especially to those who are of the household of faith.' Gal 6:10 NKJV.*

- **Forgiveness.** Again the Scripture makes this very simple. *"Bear with each other and forgive whatever grievances you may have against one another. Forgive as the Lord forgave you." Col 3:13.* If we hold any grudges as we pass through the gates of Heaven we will lose our reward. If Christ could forgive His persecutors and He lives in us, then He can give us the strength to forgive those who wound us.

Jesus parable of the unforgiving servant focuses on this very issue. Having been forgiven a great debt by the King, the servant was unwilling to forgive someone who owed him a small sum. *Matt 18:28-35 "The same servant went out, and found one of his fellow servants, which owed him an hundred pence: and he laid hands on him, and took him by the throat, saying, Pay me that which you owe. And his fellow servant fell down at his feet, and besought him, saying, Have patience with me, and I will pay thee all. And he would not: but went and cast him into prison, till he should pay the debt. So when his fellow servants saw what was* done, they were very sorry, and came and told their lord all that was done. Then his lord, after that he had called him, said unto him, O thou wicked servant, I forgave you all that debt, because you desired me to: Should you not also have had compassion on our fellow servant, even as I had pity on you? And his lord was wroth, and delivered him to the tormentors, till he should pay all that was due unto him. So likewise shall my heavenly Father do also unto you, if you do not forgive from your heart every one their trespasses." KJV modernised*

- **Finances.** What we own is not supposed to be exclusively for our benefit. Western culture is inherently greedy and self-centred. Our wealth is a trust from God to be used at His disposal. Jesus says: *"'Whoever can be trusted with very little can also be trusted with much, and whoever is dishonest with very little will also be dishonest with much. So if you have not been trustworthy in handling worldly wealth, who will trust you with true riches?" Luke 16:9-11.*

All our wealth is a trust. Do you use what you have to bless God's people now? If the answer is no, then you would not bless others if God granted you more. Do you give generously now, even if you only have a little? Then you will give generously when God trusts you with more. Many years ago I had a church member who won an amount on the foot ball pools; they came to me and genuinely said, if only we had won a little more, then we would have been able to give some to the church. Our use of money matters to heaven; it will either gain us reward or loss. *"He that sows sparingly shall reap also sparingly; and he that sows bountifully shall reap also bountifully. (Let) each man (do) according as he hath purposed in his heart: not grudgingly, or of necessity: for God loves a cheerful giver."* 2 Cor 9:6-7 ASV modernised.

Heaven does not measure things as we do; what seems of great worth here may have very little value to God. We could find that our doctrine is worth very little if we do not live out the life of Christ from the heart. I believe if under God's loving guidance, we begin to prayerfully address these areas of habits, relationships, forgiveness and finance we will not lose our reward. *'Whatever you do, work at it with all your heart, as working for the Lord, not for men, since you know that you will receive an inheritance from the Lord as a reward. It is the Lord Christ you are serving. Anyone who does wrong will be repaid for his wrong, and there is no favouritism.'* Col 3:23-25

Remember we are not talking about salvation; we are speaking about our eternal reward. It is my belief that in heaven the **spirit of a man rather than the body will be what is visible.** What we are in Christ will be clearly seen, we will be transparent before

92

God and each other. We will be forgiven, for the Judgement fell on Christ, but we will have the rank or standing that exactly fits our walk and our works. Our battle scars and the victories we have won will be evident to all. Like Jesus we will bear the wounds of triumph.

In training for reigning: Jesus promises of reigning alongside Him is only given to those who overcome. Eight times in the revelation Jesus promises honour and glory to over comers.

Rev 2:7, 'To him that overcomes will I give to eat of the tree of life, which is in the midst of the paradise of God.' KJV

Rev 2:11'He that overcomes shall not be hurt of the second death.' KJV

Rev 2:17 'To him that overcomes will I give to eat of the hidden manna.' KJV

Rev 2:26 'He that overcomes, and keeps my works unto the end, to him will I give power over the nations.' KJV

Rev 3:5 'He that overcomes, the same shall be clothed in white raiment; and I will not blot out his name out of the book of life.' KJV

Rev 3:12 'Him that overcomes will I make a pillar in the temple of my God.' KJV

Rev 3:21 'To him that overcomes will I grant to sit with me in my throne, even as I also overcame, and am set down with my Father in his throne.' KJV

Rev 21:7 'He that overcomes shall inherit all things; and I will be his God, and he shall be my son.' KJV

If we are to inherit the reward God seeks to give us **what must we do?** If we would escape judgement then God has told us to judge ourselves. *"If we would judge ourselves, we would not be judged." NKJV 1Cor 11:31.* God's call is to face and judge our sins now, so that He will not have to judge them later. What we are when we step into heaven we will be through all eternity. In order to do this we must go back to the Cross, we must face our sin and see ourselves as we really are. Then in repentance ask God to change us and make us the people He wants us to be, this is a prayer His is seeking to answer. *1 John 1:7-9 'If we walk in the light, as he is in the light, we have fellowship one with another, and the blood of Jesus Christ his Son cleanses us from all sin. If we say that we have no sin, we deceive ourselves, and the truth is not in us. If we confess our sins, he is faithful and just to forgive us our sins, and to cleanse us from all unrighteousness.' KJV.* We are called to walk in the light of God's presence, with the Spirit of God and the Word of God for our guide. When we fall we are called to come in confession and seek forgiveness. We cannot walk with God while we are walking in sin; repentance is the beginning of overcoming. Walking with the tender hand of the Holy Spirit on our conscience is the next step.

It does not matter how we look to other people, if our doctrine does not lead us into love and humility then we do not have the mind or nature of Christ. What is valued with men is of very little value in heaven. That is why we are told, *"Many who are first will be last, and the last first." Mark 10:31.* How we build our lives upon the rock of Christ has eternal consequences.

There is a judgement seat for Christians and in that day what we are will be brought to light. The *"day will bring it to light. It will be revealed with fire, and the fire will test the quality of each man's work. If what he has built survives, he will receive his reward. If it is burned up, he will suffer loss; he himself will be saved, but only as one escaping through the flames." 1 Cor 3:13-15*

Our standing in heaven depends on our faith, our obedience and our attitude today. By God's grace each of us can be an over comer. For, *"We must all appear before the judgement seat of Christ, that each one may receive what is due to him for the things done while in the body, whether good or bad." 2 Cor 5:10.*

A Prayer: Father I understand that my sins cause pain to your heart. Sometimes I am so attached to my sin, teach me to judge my wrong attitudes and actions so that you will not have to judge me. Show me how to walk in humility and make me a lover of your people. Grant that I may become an over comer in Jesus' name. Amen.

Study Questions.

1. What do we mean by the term the fear of the Lord?

2. Describe the two different judgements.

3. Look up: Luke 16: 1-13 and Luke 19:112-19 and then talk about the principle of proportional reward.

4. When we stand before God will our sins cause us shame?

5. Why will some Christians be saved but have no reward?

6. What attitude was in Christ?

7. What is the true badge of a Christian? Describe its opposite attitude?

8. What two things are we called to obey?

9. What is the danger in obedience?

10. What do we mean by 'religion has a, can't do attitude'?

11. Do we cling to any attitudes of the Pharisee?

12. Where is our doctrine supposed to lead us?

13. Have we made a truce with any of our sins?

14. If we will be judged on how our relationships are lived out, what should we do about it?

15. Is there anyone you need to forgive?

16. Remember giving is done in secret, when did you last bless one of God's people?

17. What does God ask us to do to avoid judgement?

Further readings: Matt 25:31-46, Rev Ch 20, Philippians Ch 2.

Appendix: Hebrews 4v4-11.

Sabbath rest explained.

In Hebrews 4:4-11, God's rest is described as a Sabbath rest and this brings three images to mind.

To enter the Sabbath rest is to *share in the rest of God* (v4). God himself has been at rest since He completed creation (see v3-4). The creation account in Genesis emphasises this thought. On each day of creation, God reviewed His achievement, pronounced it good and then the day closed (e.g. Gen 1:18+19 *and God saw that it was good. And there was evening and there was morning the fourth day.*) Each day follows this pattern except for the last or seventh day. On the sixth day, He proclaims the creation to be very good and blesses it. On the seventh, He rests from all His work. *"And blessed the seventh day and made it holy"* (Gen 2:2-3). But there is no evening or morning; **the day of rest never closes.** On that day God entered into His rest, a rest of satisfaction at a job well done. God now rests as Lord over creation. He is un-perturbed by our rebellion for He knows how creation will unfold and is satisfied with His work. From day seven to Kingdom come, He rests in perfect peace and contentment. God is confident in His creation and supremely confident in the final outcome of all things. This confidence gives us the pattern of the first rest we are offered.

Three types of rest: - Creation rest, Salvation rest, and Heavenly rest.

Creation rest: This pattern of six days' work and one day rest is woven into the fabric of creation. When we ignore our need for rest and re-creation, we will lose our peace of mind and even become ill. Six days' work, one day for rest and reflection: a Holy Day, a day to review our accomplishments and to hand them back to God; a day when we acknowledge that all our hopes and aspirations come by God's help and by God's grace, a day to see the smallness of the creature and the greatness of the Creator. This pattern became an eternal principle in the Ten Commandments. Exodus 20:8-11 *"remember the Sabbath day by keeping it holy, six days you shall labour and do all your work, but the seventh is a Sabbath to the Lord your God. On it you shall not do any work ----For in six days the Lord made the heavens and the earth, the sea and all that is in them, but he rested on the seventh. Therefore the Lord blessed the Sabbath day and made it holy"*. A natural rest is built into the order of creation. Learning to accept this rest brings order and harmony to a chaotic lifestyle. This day of rest refreshes us physically, spiritually and psychologically; we ignore it at our peril, for we are created to rest one day in seven.

The Sabbath rest is no longer an obligation; we are not to be enslaved by what we can do and cannot do on the Sabbath. Jesus said clearly that *"The Sabbath was made for man, not man for the Sabbath. So the Son of Man is Lord even of the Sabbath."* *Mark 2:27-28.* The Sabbath day principle shows that our priorities are not mammon but God. It is a principle, something created for our spiritual and psychological good. The Pharisees who regulated everything that you could do on a Sabbath forgot that you could still do good on the Sabbath. A good rule is can you invite Jesus to do it with you? Yet this is only the first form of Sabbath rest.

When we look at **Salvation rest**, verse ten is the key to our understanding: *"Anyone who enters Gods' rest also rests from his own work".* This is a rest which cannot be earned or achieved by our own works. It is a gift of God, given in response to faith. Our works however good or noble can only bring the acclaim of man, but never the blessing of God. When we seek salvation, someone else has to do it for us. We must *"rest from our own works."* The King James Version helps us here: *"He that is entered into his rest, he also has rested from his own works".* The 'He' referred to here is a specific person: HE is Jesus, and He alone can bring us into Salvation rest. He came with a specific task to accomplish and as Priest and sacrifice, He finished the work of salvation (Heb2:17). On His ascension He entered into His rest and now He rests in the knowledge of a job well done. On the Cross, the cry: *"it is finished"* rang out. Christ's work of Salvation is complete, our works can add nothing to it, and if we would enter into this rest we must accept Salvation as a work of Christ. In Salvation we receive freely a gift we could never earn, we must rest from our own works. Christ Himself put it in these terms: *"Come to me, all you who are weary and burdened, and I will give you rest. Take my yolk upon you and learn from me, for I am gentle and humble in heart, and you will find rest for your souls".* *(Mt 11:27-28)*

Jesus is the mediator of a new covenant says Hebrews (12:24). This rest comes through entering into this covenant, from our being united through faith to Jesus, the one who earned salvation rest. This rest is **a tangible spiritual assurance** that enters the soul and it can deepen over the years. It is through faith that we enter into this rest; it is by obeying God and growing in our faith that His rest enters into us. This rest is in essence a sharing in the confidence of Jesus. We are confident that regardless of our own work, all Jesus has done for our salvation is enough. Such a rest begins now and continues into eternity. Traditionally Methodists call this rest Assurance! This rest is worth finding.

We should be diligent about our faith, not treating it as a light or insignificant thing, but make every effort to enter this rest, ensuring our own disobedience does not exclude us (v11).

The third picture of Sabbath rest is of our final or **heavenly rest**. Our life on earth should be seen as the six days of work in the creation narrative. At the end, we will step into the presence of God and share His heavenly rest. *"His master replied, well done good and faithful servant! You have been faithful with a few things; I will put you in charge of many things. Come and share in your master's happiness" (Mt25:21)*

Christian rest **works then on three levels**. On the natural level, we receive the wisdom to live a life which focuses on God's goodness; it draws strength from Him and sets aside one day in seven to build that relationship. On the Spiritual level, we cease from striving for salvation and allow the rest that Christ brings to enter our souls, trusting his work on the Cross to guarantee our salvation. In the future, through God's promises, we will enter our Heavenly rest, where we will share God's eternal confidence.

Bibliography.

Hession, Roy. *The Calvary Road.* (CLC, 1995 ed)

Hughes, Selwyn. *7 laws of spiritual Success*, (CWR 2008)
                 Why Revival Waits, (CWR 2003)
                 Christ Empowered Living, (CWR 2002)
                 Learning to Care, (CWR 1996.)

Joyner, Rick. *The Final Quest,* (Whitaker House, 1996)

Lewis C. S. *Mere Christianity*, (Fount Books, 1952)

Lucado, M. *In the Eye of the Storm*, (Word publishing, 1991)

Electronic Bible reference *PC Study Bible* V3.1 C1993 - 2000

Bible quotations are from the Authorised Version 1611

The New King James Nelson Publishing 1982

The Holy Bible: New International Version. Copyright (c) 1973, 1978, 1984, by International Bible Society unless otherwise stated.

Cover portrait from the Sistine Chapel creation of Adam from freechristimages.org

What are your hot poker principles?

1.

2.

3.

4.

5.

6.

7.

8.

9.

10.

Jude 24-25: Now unto him that is able to keep you from falling, and to present you faultless before the presence of his glory with exceeding joy, to the only wise God our Saviour, be glory and majesty, dominion and power, both now and ever. Amen. KJV

Page for making notes.

Page for making notes.

Page for making notes.

Lightning Source UK Ltd.
Milton Keynes UK
UKHW02f2245110418
320897UK00005B/280/P